CREDIT WISE

The Definitive 12-Step Guide to Repairing Your Credit

By

Dr. Derek Smith, Ed.D, MBA, MS
Certified Financial Consultant, Certified Financial
Planner, and Certified Credit Repair Specialist

First Edition 2020

ISBN-9798690305482

Simplified Financial Services LLC

www.simplifiedfinancialservices.com

Dedication

This book is dedicated to my wife Andrea, my wonderful daughters Jaime, and the twins Mackenzie and Madison. I also want to thank my mentors, who's advice and guidance have helped me build and grow my financial business. Thank you, Dominique Brown and Alexa Fleury-Leonard, for your guidance, inspiration, and mentorship. Which has made this book possible by providing me with experiences and the knowledge needed to build my businesses.

THE IDEAL PROFESSIONAL SPEAKER FOR YOUR NEXT EVENT

Derek will captivate your audience while discussing important financial topics. Hire Derek for your next a keynote and/or workshop today!

TO CONTACT OR BOOK DEREK FOR SPEAKING OR TRAINING ENGAGEMENTS:

301 744-7355

derek@ncseonline.com

CONTENTS

Preface

Why I wrote this book!

As an educator, financial planner and coach, I saw a need to provide the many people suffering with a low credit score a means to work towards improving their credit and subsequently their score.

The Credit Bureaus often make mistakes on credit reports and these mistakes can prove detrimental to you when you are doing such activities as buying a home or a car. Your credit score can even determine where you live or where your children can go to school, and even where you work.

This guide will provide you with the knowledge and tools (in the form of letters) you need to fix your own credit. After reading it you will be fully prepared to fix your credit.

However, fixing your credit can be hard and if you ever need assistance you can visit my sites at www.comprehensivecreditrepair.com or www.simplifiedfinancialservices or contact me at derek@comprehensivefinancialservices.com or derek@simplifiedfinancialservices.com

Sincerely

Dr. Derek A. Smith

PART ONE – INTRODUCTION

What Is Credit Repair

Credit Repair may be an unfamiliar term for many people. Its meaning is simple: It is the process of cleaning up your credit report by learning how to remove unwanted information, such as false, outdated, or unverified information. Many consumers are not fully aware of laws that protect them. They include The Fair Credit Reporting Act (FCRA) and the Fair Debt Collection Practices Act (FDCPA).

With patience and a little education, Which I about to give you, you can learn about your rights and utilize them to improve your credit report and score and protect yourself from harassment from creditors and debt collectors.

The Regulations

The Fair Credit Reporting Act, passed in 1970, ensures that Consumer Reporting Agencies (CRA's) report only accurate and verifiable information to your credit report. Credit report errors are a common occurrence, so consumers must be diligent about monitoring their credit reports. As a consumer, you have the right to request an investigation if you find information on your credit report to be inaccurate. Once your request is received, a CRA has a limited amount of time to complete the investigation. If the CRA fails to meet the deadline, The FCRA requires that the item in question be removed. The FDCPA outlines practices by creditors to collect that are acceptable, as well as those that are illegal. Educating yourself about how creditors are allowed and not allowed to collect a debt can help raise your awareness and avoid having debt collected unfairly. Working knowledge of both these acts will help you repair your credit and ensure you are treated fairly by creditors.

Ethical Credit Repair

It is important to remember that credit repair is designed to remove only information that is inaccurate or outdated. It is unethical to use the credit repair process to remove real and accurate information from your credit report. In addition, it is crucial to understand that removing items from your credit report does not exempt you from debt that you legally owe. Once you have an item removed, you can work with the creditor to arrange a settlement offer or payment arrangement. Doing so can prevent your debt from being sold to another collection agency who will report it again in the future. As you utilize the steps and tools outlined in this book, please keep your own ethical and financial responsibility in mind, and you will see your credit scores improve.

Organization is the Key to Your Success

Before you begin writing dispute letters to the bureaus, you must first organize yourself and your information. To succeed with credit repair, it is imperative to create a system to record, track, and store your correspondence. Being aware of and tracking deadlines that credit bureaus must meet is the first step. Learn these deadlines and record them. Be mindful of your rights and the next steps if the bureaus do not meet their deadlines. Of equal importance are deadlines that you, as the consumer, must meet. Once you have sent correspondence, record the date it was sent and the Bureau's deadline. Use certified mail so you will have confirmation that your correspondence has been received. Keep a record of all correspondence for each dispute. Record keeping on your part is essential.

WHAT YOU NEED

- Manila Folders

- Calendar or Calendar App

- Creditor List (page...)

- Double Window Envelopes

- Certified Mail Tags

- A Printer

LABEL YOUR FOLDERS

- Credit Reports Folder 1 - In this folder, you will put your 3 bureau reports only.

- Miscellaneous Folder - You can store letters and responses sent regarding inquiries and personal info correction in this folder.

- Equifax Reports - Put the reports you get from Equifax when they respond to your letter in this folder.

- Experian Reports - Put the reports you get from Experian when they respond to your letter in this folder.

- TransUnion Reports - Put the reports you get from TransUnion when they respond to your letter in this folder.

- Bureau Set 1 - You will dispute 5 accounts with the bureaus at one time. Store this first set in one folder. It will include your letters, as well as their responses.

- Bureau Set 2 - (next 5 creditors)

- One for Each Creditor - if the account is not removed after your first letter to the Bureau, set up a folder for the individual creditors. You will store the letters you write to them and their responses in their own folder.

PART TWO - THE LAWS

CONSUMER LAW

Consumer law encompasses the mass of laws and regulations set forth by various government agencies to protect consumers from unfair and/or predatory practices. In the case of credit repair, the most important applicable regulations and laws are the Fair Credit Reporting Act, the Fair Debt Collection Practices Act, and the Fair Credit Billing Act. Let's discuss those regulations together.

Consumer law falls under a broad umbrella of regulations covered by the Fair Credit Reporting Act, the Fair Debt Collection Practices Act, and the Fair Credit Billing Act. These are the most essential acts to utilize for credit repair. Below is a summary of each.

FAIR CREDIT REPORTING ACT

The Fair Credit Reporting Act is designed to regulate how CRA's can collect, record, and report on consumer credit files. The three main CRA's, Experian, Equifax, and TransUnion, must adhere to standards outlined in the FCRA. Lenders and financial institutions use consumer files purchased from the three main CRA's to evaluate a consumer's loan risk; it is imperative that the information is reported accurately and has been verified. If CRA's do not meet the standards, the FCRA requires them to remove information not verified or accurate.

FAIR DEBT COLLECTION PRACTICES ACT

The Fair Debt Collection Practices Act was passed as an amendment to the Consumer Protections Act in 1977 and was intended to protect consumers from unfair practices by debt collectors and creditors.

FAIR CREDIT BILLING ACT

The Fair Credit Billing Act, passed in 1974, protects consumers from unethical or illegal billing practices by creditors.

PART THREE - UNDERSTANDING YOUR REPORTS

Credit Reporting Agencies

CRA's are the companies with whom you will file requests and/or disputes.

A Credit Reporting Agency (CRA) is a company that compiles and sells credit reports. CRAs collect data about consumers, including loan status, credit card balances, payment status on accounts, items sent for collection, and public records such as judgments, liens, and bankruptcies. They collect information from lenders, public records, and collection agencies. The three main CRA's are often referred to as the Credit Bureaus.

The Fair and Accurate Credit Transactions Act allows consumers to receive and review their credit reports free of charge once a year.

Breaking Down Your Credit Report

What IS and ISN'T on your credit report.

<u>Information included on your credit report:</u>

- Personal Identifiers

- Public Records

- Inquiries

- Credit Accounts

- Collection Accounts

<u>Information not included on your credit report:</u>

- Your income

- Your Bank Accounts

- Your Credit Score

Personal Information

Because this section of your report contains your personal identifiers, you must monitor it for accuracy. Errors often occur in this section. It includes your name, date of birth, social security number, current and past addresses and phone numbers, and employers that have been reported to the bureaus through your creditors.

It is believed that by removing old addresses, accounts under those addresses may be removed more quickly using the bureaus' automated dispute program.

For instructions to remove or correct personal information, refer to the index on the next page.

Inquiries

There is a section labeled "Inquiries" on your credit report.

Removing inquiries from your report can increase your score by several points per removal. Before we get into how to do that, let us first discuss what inquiries are, and the differences between a hard inquiry and a soft inquiry.

Inquiries into your credit information can decrease your credit score, so removing them is one step in increasing that score. Below is a summary of the two kinds of inquiries found on a credit report.

Hard Inquiries

Hard inquiries are those made by creditors to evaluate your credit when you apply for a loan, mortgage, car loan, or credit card. After each inquiry, an entry will be added to your credit file showing the lender's information. These types of inquiries have a slightly negative effect on your credit and will remain there for two years. After one year, they no longer negatively affect your score. Disputing inquiries is only worth your energy if they are less than a year old.

A lender must have your permission to pull your credit file and must have a permissible purpose.

Soft Inquiries

To make a soft inquiry, a lender does not need your permission. This is because soft inquires do not appear on your credit report or affect your credit score. They are usually used for promotional purposes.

Public Record

These can be found on your reports under the section labeled "Public Record."

Matters of public record often appear in a credit file. They include bankruptcies, liens, and judgments against you. Often this information is uncovered by third party information sellers who sell it to the bureaus. It is possible to remove these types of items. Methods will be explained later in the book.

Account History

The two main types of accounts found in a credit file are **Credit Accounts and Collection Accounts**. This section of your credit report is where you begin to search for errors, such as outdated, inaccurate, or unverifiable information. Information in this section is provided by lenders and/or collection agencies.

Credit Accounts

Credit accounts are the accounts (positive or negative) that are being reported directly by your lenders. They will list:

- Lender's Name

- Partial Account Number

- Date Opened

- Account Type

- Date of Last Payment

- Date Last Reported

- Date of Last Activity

- Amount Owed

- Pay Status (Current/Late)

- Credit Limit

- High Credit

- Payment History

Collection Accounts

Collection accounts are those sold or placed with a third party for collection. They will include the following information:

- Agency Name

- Partial Account Number

- Date Opened

- Account Type

- Date of Last Payment

- Date Last Reported

- Amount Owed

Since the name of the original creditor is not always provided, you will need to contact the collection agency to obtain that information.

What Is A Credit Score?

The system for calculating a credit score was devised by companies like FICO and Vantage scores and involves a complex algorithm. The algorithm produces a numeric value designed to rate your credit worthiness. Because each of the three credit bureaus collects and records data independently, your score may vary between bureaus. Because a credit score is based on a person's unique information, there is a considerable variation of scores among the population.

Understanding Your Score

The five categories on your credit score are each weighted differently.

- 35% Payment History

- 30% Credit Utilization

- 15 % Credit Age

- 10% New Credit

- 10% Credit Mix

Payment History

The category with the largest weight on your credit score is payment history. Keeping up to date on payments owed is key to maintaining the credit score you desire. According to FICO, just one late payment on an account can drop your score anywhere from 90-110 points. Creditors will report your payments to the bureaus monthly. The later the payment, the more your score will drop.

Credit Utilization

Credit Utilization is the second most substantial influence on your credit score. Credit utilization compares the percentage of your credit limits used and the percentage of payments still owed versus the income you earn.

Credit Age

Credit age takes into account several factors, including the oldest account, the age of specific accounts, and when accounts were last used. It is also known as **length of history** and accounts for 15% of your score.

Credit mix

Credit mix looks at the type of credit accounts you have, including revolving accounts, installment accounts, retail accounts, and auto loans and mortgages. Maintaining a balanced mix is good for your credit file.

New Credit

Account age has an influence on your credit history. The longer you hold an account and make payments regularly, the better. New accounts lower your average account age and can have a more significant impact on your scores, especially if you don't have a lot of other credit information in your file. When you open a new account, it is essential to build a positive payment history quickly. 10% of your credit score is based on new credit.

Verification Vs. Validation

Now that you have a better understanding of what is on your credit report, let's discuss the two ways to combat incorrect, erroneous, and unverifiable information.

The verification process is done directly with the Credit Bureaus

When the Bureaus receive information from furnishers, they must verify that it is true and accurate. In doing so, they must follow the regulations and procedures described in The Fair Credit Reporting Act. The FCRA also requires that information be removed from your file if any of the three bureaus does not follow its regulations during the verification process. Diligence on your part in monitoring the Bureau's record-keeping in your file can help you have unverified or inaccurate information removed.

The validation process is done directly with the Creditors.

Validation is the expectation that the creditors will have to prove that you actually owe the debt. They will often send you a copy of the bill, but a bill doesn't mean you opened the account or agreed to the responsibility of the debt. They must provide you with a contract from the original creditor or some equally iron clad proof that you agreed to the debt. If they do not or cannot provide this, then they are required to remove the file from your credit report.

Like the bureaus, creditors are required to validate information that proves you opened an account or agreed to a responsibility of debt. This includes not only a copy of a bill but also a copy of the contract or agreement from the original creditor as documentation. Creditors unable to validate such information are required to remove it from your file.

PART FOUR - 12 Steps to Repairing Your Credit

STEP ONE - OBTAIN A CREDIT REPORT

Obtaining a copy of your credit report is the first step in the credit repair process. Luckily, this is an easy step.

Passed in 2003, The Fair Credit Transactions Act allows you free access to your credit report annually from each of the three bureaus.

Luckily, this is an easy step. Simply go to: www.annualcreditreport.com.

While repairing your credit report, you will need access more often than once a year. Signing up for a monthly credit monitoring service is the best way to do it.

Simplify your document process: Get your CREDIT SCORE and CREDIT REPORT from the same website available from our affiliate here:

Identity IQ - https://www.identityiq.com/help-you-to-save-money.aspx?offercode=431252GY

Smart Credit -

http://www.smartcredit.com/comprehensivecreditrepair

STEP TWO - BREAK DOWN YOUR ACCOUNTS

Once you have broken down all the accounts in your credit history by listing and recording them, you can begin the letter-writing process.

The next few pages will allow you to organize your account information by filling out worksheets with the pertinent information. This information will be used when you get to the letter-writing phase. These letters will be sent to the bureaus and your creditors.

Your Personal Information

Review Your credit report and list all negative accounts here.

This is the information you will include in your DISPUTE letters.

1. **Are there names you do not recognize?**

2. **Are there other dates of birth?**

3. **Is your Social Security Number correct?**

4. Are the erroneous/old addresses listed?

5. Do you want your phone number listed?

What names need to be deleted:

1.

2.

3.

4.

What DOB's need to be deleted:

1.

2.

3.

4.

What Social Security Numbers need to be deleted:

1.

2.

3.

4.

What addresses need to be deleted:

1.

2.

3.

4.

5.

6.

7.

8.

9.

10.

What phone numbers need to be deleted:

1.

2.

3.

4.

5.

6.

7.

8.

9.

10.

Your Inquiries

Review Your credit report and list all inquiries that are less than 12 months old here

CREDITORS   **DATE**   **REPORTED**

    1. .

    2. .

    3. .

    4. .

    5. .

    6. .

    7. .

    8. .

    9. .

    10. .

11. .

12. .

13. .

14. .

15. .

16. .

17. .

18. .

19. .

20. .

21. .

22. .

23. .

24. .

Your Negative Accounts

Creditor Acct# DOLP AMT OWED DLR

1. .

2. .

3. .

4. .

5. .

6. .

7. .

8. .

9. .

10. .

11. .

12. .

13. .

14. .

15. .

16. .

17. .

18. .

19. .

20. .

21. .

22. .

23. .

24. .

25. .

STEP THREE - CORRECTING PERSONAL INFORMATION

Send the Corresponding Letters from the Letter Index on Page 74 to correct personal information

	To Whom	When
Letter #1	**Credit Bureaus**	**Day 1**
Sometimes the Bureau will respond and try to tell you that you need to correct the addresses associated with accounts on your file and state that they should be updated by the furnisher. This is simply not true. Send Letter # 2!		
Letter #2	**Credit Bureaus**	**When Letter # 1 Does not result in removal**

STEP FOUR - INQUIRY REMOVAL

Send the Corresponding Letters from the Letter Index on page 74 to remove inquiries

	To Whom	When
Letter # 3	Credit Bureaus	Day 1
Letter # 4	Data Furnishers/ Creditors	When Letter # 3 Does Not result in removal
Letter # 5	Credit Bureaus	At the same time, you send #4
Letter # 6	Data Furnishers/ Creditors	If Letter #4 Does not result in removal

STEP FIVE - CORRECT PAYMENT HISTORY

Credit Utilization and Payment History make up 65% of your credit score. These are the first areas to address in the credit repair process.

Start by reaching out to your creditors for a listing of late payments reported in the last 18 months. Check over the list to make sure all the payments were actually late. If they were, you can request a goodwill adjustment.

Next, develop a plan to reduce any balances that are higher than 30% of your credit limit. Following through on the plan can help increase your credit score more quickly.

Follow the directions and worksheets on the next pages to track and record your activity.

LATE PAYMENTS

If you have late payments with a creditor, you can request a transaction history to check against your bank records. It is important to keep in mind that a creditor cannot identify a payment as 30 days late until the 31st day after the bill due date. If your examination of your records reveals that your payments were late, you can request a goodwill removal, along with a promise to put the account on autopay. This can improve your chances of reaching an agreement with the creditor.

	To Whom	What Letter
Letter # 7	Data Furnisher/ Creditor	Request Transaction History
Letter # 8	Data Furnisher/ Creditor	Goodwill Letter

Creditor:		
Equifax	Experian	Transunion
1.		
2.		
3.		
4.		
5.		

Creditor:		
Equifax	Experian	Transunion
1.		
2.		
3.		
4.		
5.		

Creditor:		
Equifax	Experian	Transunion
1.		
2.		
3.		
4.		
5.		

Creditor:		
Equifax	**Experian**	**Transunion**
1.		
2.		
3.		
4.		
5.		
Creditor:		
Equifax	**Experian**	**Transunion**
1.		
2.		
3.		
4.		
5.		
Creditor:		
Equifax	**Experian**	**Transunion**
1.		
2.		
3.		
4.		
5.		

LATE PAYMENT LOG

STEP SIX - REDUCE UTILIZATION

Credit utilization reflects the percentage of your credit limit you are currently using. Keeping that percentage below 30 is a good target for reducing the negative impact credit utilization can have on your score.

Ideally, it is best to keep your credit utilization at 1-2%. Build up to this goal by aiming for 10-15% first and gradually working toward 1-2%. Using your cards regularly and making timely payments can also help build your score.

UTILIZATION WORKSHEET

Review your file and list the revolving accounts (Accounts with credit limits) Along with their balances and what you need to pay to reduce to 30% or 15%

Creditor:

____

Credit Limit:

Balance:

% Utilization:

Reduce to 30%:

Reduce to 15%:

Creditor:

____

Credit Limit:

Balance:

% Utilization:

Reduce to 30%:

Reduce to 15%:

Creditor:

Credit Limit:

Balance:

% Utilization:

Reduce to 30%:

Reduce to 15%:

Creditor:

Credit Limit:

Balance:

% Utilization:

Reduce to 30%:

Reduce to 15%:

Creditor:

Credit Limit:

Balance:

% Utilization:

Reduce to 30%:

Reduce to 15%:

Creditor:

____

Credit Limit:

Balance:

% Utilization:

Reduce to 30%:

Reduce to 15%:

Creditor:

____

Credit Limit:

Balance:

% Utilization:

Reduce to 30%:

Reduce to 15%:

STEP SEVEN - APPLY POSITIVE ACCOUNTS

A positive account is one that you use and make payments on regularly. Because payment history is 35% of your credit score, the positive accounts you maintain, the better your credit will be.

On the following page, you will find resources for opening accounts to build your credit with no credit or damaged credit.

To keep your file diverse but responsible, we recommend the following mix of accounts:

- 3 Revolving Accounts (Credit Cards)
- 2 Retail Accounts (Store Cards)
- 1-2 Installment Accounts (loans, auto loans, etc.)
- Mortgage Account

Additional Reportable Items:

- Rent
- Utilities

(On the following page, list your own affiliate relationships with places like Fingerhut, self lender, myjewlersclub, newcoast direct, and other credit card companies you affiliate with. I did not put in a mock page for this)

STEP EIGHT - DISPUTING WITH THE CREDIT REPORTING AGENCIES

Now it's time to start Disputing accounts with the credit bureaus

E-Oscar is an optical character recognition program provided to Data Furnishers by the three credit bureaus. This program isn't always reliable in meeting compliance with FCRA standards for credit investigations. This unreliability can be used to leverage the removal of unverifiable information from credit reports.

Where to Send disputes

You can send your request and copies of documents to the three nationwide credit bureaus at the following addresses:

Equifax Information Services, LLC

P.O. Box 740256

Atlanta, GA 30374-0256

Experian

P.O. Box 4500

Allen, TX 75013

TransUnion Consumer Solutions

P.O. Box 2000

Chester, PA 19016

The Process

As mentioned before, your folder organization system is a vital tool in disputing credit information. Before starting the dispute process, be sure it is ready to go. Be prepared to record deadlines on your calendar as well.

There are nine letters in total. For each letter, the process and steps will be explained. Although it is difficult to predict the results, your organization, persistence, and diligence will be the key to your success.

Start with your first five derogatory accounts. If you have more than five, you will need to stagger them over time, sending a letter for the next five every two weeks. This will prevent the bureaus from labeling your disputes as frivolous. Consult the timeline on page 50 for a more detailed explanation.

	What Accounts	**When**
Letter # 9	**First 5 Negative Accounts**	Day 1
Letter # 9	**Next 5 Negative Accounts**	Day 14
Letter # 9	**Next 5 Negative Accounts**	Day 21

Every two weeks, send out Letter #7 for each new group of five accounts you are disputing.

- The FCRA requires bureaus to complete the investigation into the dispute within 30 days of receiving your letter.

- If you send in any additional information about your initial dispute, the deadline is extended from 30 to 45 days.

- Use certified mail so that you will have the date they received your letter, as well as the date they sent their return letter and the postmark date.

Responding to Stall Letters

Because they receive almost 20,000 letters a day, the bureaus may be behind schedule. You may receive letters that claim you have not provided enough information. Examples are listed below.

Four of the most common ways the bureaus stall:

- Claim you didn't send enough proof of ID, when in fact, you did.

- Claim they could not locate your file with the information you provided.

- Claim they do not believe it was you who wrote the letter.

- Claiming your investigation is frivolous.

Using the index section of this book, you will find 4 letters to respond to these stall tactics.

- Letter #10 - Not Enough ID provide

- Letter #11 - could not Locate file

- Letter #12 - Don't BELIEVE it was you

- Letter #13 - Frivolous Disputing

If the Bureaus Fail to Respond

Within 30 days, you should have a response from the Bureau. If you have not received a response after 45 days, that is a violation of the FCRA. You can hold the Bureau accountable for that.

The FCRA states they have 30 days from the date the letter was received to complete the investigation.

- They may have up to 45 days if and ONLY if you have mailed in additional information AFTER the initial dispute letter.

- Because you used certified mail, you will have a record of when your letter was received and when the Bureau's response was sent.

Your next step is to compose a letter to the Bureau stating that they have not met the 30-day requirement as outlined in the FCRA. Because they violate the FCRA, they are required to remove the account(s) from your credit report. Inform the Bureau that you are aware that you have the right to request that they remove the information from your credit report and explain your intention to sue if they do not comply.

If the Bureau responds and the account was not deleted

If you do receive a response to your dispute within 30 days and the Bureau informs you that the account was verified as accurate and belongs to you, you still have a right to request that the Bureau verify its method of verification. You may formally request to be informed of the Bureau's Method of Verification (MOV).

- FCRA 611 (a)(6) and (7) states you have a right to request their method of verification

- The Bureau must respond to the MOV request within 15 days.

	What Accounts	When
Letter # 14	Each Set of 5	Within 5 Days of Receiving a Response

If the Bureau Fails the MOV Process

FCRA 611 (a)(6) and (7) states they only have 15 days to respond. Use your certified mail receipts to track the amount of time. If 15 days pass with no response, you may now:

- File a complaint with the Consumer Financial Protection Bureau at www.consumerfianance.gov and provide them with proof of correspondence.

- Attach that to Letter #16 and send it to the bureaus that failed to provide Method of Verification.

	What Accounts	**When**
Letter # 15	**Each Set of 5**	**Within 5 Days of Receiving a Response**

If the bureaus still fail to remove the account

Disclaimer: I am not an attorney and are not giving legal advice. At this stage in the process, we highly recommend an affordable account with Legal Shield or another consumer protection attorney.

If you decide to pursue this dispute further because the Bureau has not met the 15-day deadline, you do have a right to go to your local court and file a small claims action. A letter has been provided in the index for your use.

	What Accounts	When
Letter # 16	Each Set of 5	Within 5 Days of Receiving a Response

STEP NINE - CRUSHING THE CREDITORS

Another effective avenue you can pursue is to dispute information in your credit report directly with your creditors.

If you have not experienced success with your second round of letters with the credit bureaus, you may begin sending letters directly to your creditors. This section will outline the process to follow.

Validation

The FDCPA outlines requirements for validation of information, but they can be vague and unclear. However, the burden of proof lies with the creditors, rather than the consumer. A judge is likely to require the creditor to provide undeniable and verifiable evidence that the debt belongs to you. By communicating to creditors, the need for them to provide evidence that would hold up in court, it is possible to force the data furnisher to remove the report if they are not able to comply.

The most common response from data furnishers is a bill. However, it is important to keep in mind that anyone can open an account in your name, so a bill does not necessarily prove that the debt belongs to you. Continue to pressure the creditor for more substantial evidence, such as a contract with the original creditor bearing your signature, demonstrating your agreement to pay the debt. In the absence of this evidence, it is unlikely that the court would rule in favor of the creditor. If it is clear to you before going to court that the creditor will not be able to provide sufficient evidence of your agreement to pay the debt, it would be fair to push for the debt to be removed from your credit file.

The Process

To start the validation process with the Bureau, you must first send a validation request to the creditor. Send this letter directly to the creditor at the address they are reporting to your credit file. Pro Tip: If the letter comes back as undelivered, send a copy of that to the Bureau, and they will remove the report due to not reporting true and accurate information.

	What Letter	**When**
Letter # 17	**Validation Letter**	**At the same time, you send MOV on to the Bureau on this account.**
Letter # 18	**If They Respond Without Contracts**	**Within 5 Days of Receiving Their Letter**
Letter # 19	**If They Do Not Respond After 30 Days**	**Within 5 Days of Receiving Their Letter**
Letter # 20	**If They Respond Again Without Contracts**	**Within 5 Days of Receiving Their Letter**

Creditors and collection agencies must mark the account as disputed in your credit file within 30 days of receiving your letter (remember your old friend, certified mail!). On the 31st day, check your credit report and print it with a timestamp included. If the account was not reported as disputed, it must be removed from your credit file.

Small Claims

If you haven't received a response or validation of information from a creditor, your next step is to sue in small claims court.

I am not an attorney, and this is not legal advice. You should always consult an attorney when considering legal action.

Since you have exercised your rights under consumer law and not received the required response from the creditor, it's time for the next step: suing the creditor.

Consult with an attorney, or go down to the courthouse and file a small claims lawsuit. Attach it to Letter #16 in the index, replacing with the creditor's address, and send it through certified mail.

It may be less expensive for a data furnisher to delete the account and cease collection rather than traveling to your area to appear in court. This outcome is possible. However, if the case does go to court, an attorney may be able to show how the company violated your rights and seek relief in the form of dismissing the debt and paying damages to you. Again, results vary, and I suggest legal counsel.

STEP TEN - NAVIGATING A REPOSSESSION

Lenders are required to follow specific laws when they repossess your vehicle. They often fail to follow the process legally, especially when it comes to providing the correct paperwork.

The Cure Notice

In most states, after a car repossession, the lender is required to allow you to cure the default and redeem your vehicle. Lenders are required to provide you with a notice explaining the total amount needed to redeem your car, including any fees uncured. Understanding your state laws is imperative. The more knowledge you have, the more leverage you will have. Along with the notice regarding redeeming your car, some states also include a notice of their intent to sell your vehicle. This notice may come separately. Ensure that you and any co-signer on your car loan received such notification 10 days before the sale or auction.

The Notice of Sale should include:

- A description of the vehicle

- The date, time, and place the vehicle is being sold

- Whether it was an auction or private sale

- A notice that you are allowed to review any accounting documents and the contact information to do so.

The Deficiency Notice

Once your car is sold or auctioned off, the lender must send a notice of sale that includes the sale amount, a listing of what you owe to cover repossession costs, as well as the amount owed for the difference between what you owe on the loan and the sale price. Although it happens rarely, if the care was sold for more than what you owe, you may be entitled to the difference.

You also may be able to contest the amount the lenders claims you owe if the vehicle was sold at an unreasonably low cost. According to the claim Uniform Commercial Code, N.J.S.A. 12A: 9-610(b), the lender is not entitled to all of the money it seeks if the sale was not commercially reasonable, making the sale price unreasonably low. In the case, either side sues the other, and your claim is successful, the court may award you damages under N.J.S.A. 12A:9-625, which could reduce or eliminate the amount you owe.

The Process

Your first step in the process is to send the letter a request for specific information, which they are unlikely to be able to provide. Although repossessions are not often removed, an attempt to do so is encouraged. After you receive a response from the lender, you can send a series of two letters, one to the creditor and one to the Bureau.

It is crucial to keep in mind that due to the large amounts of money usually owed on repossessions, it is possible that the creditor may initiate a lawsuit, whether you dispute the account or not. Therefore, it is recommended that you wait until the statute of limitations for your state has passed before you initiate the dispute process.

	What Letter	When
Letter # 21	Lender	Day 1
Letter # 22	Lender	Within 5 Days of Receiving Their Letter
Letter # 23	Lender	20 Days After They Receive Letter #21

STEP Eleven - Deleting Bankruptcy

Removing a bankruptcy from all three bureaus is an extremely difficult task. Conversely, recovering from a bankruptcy is not as lengthy and difficult process as you might think. A good strategy is to build 12-24 months of positive and responsible credit history. This will make it more likely that lenders will be willing to overlook bankruptcy when evaluating your credit worthiness for a loan.

The Process

Before you can begin disputing bankruptcy public records, you will need to review your credit report to make sure all appropriate accounts are listed correctly under the bankruptcy category. The first step is to look for accounts that were included in your bankruptcy but not categorized as such on your report. These accounts will not have "bankruptcy status" listed in the notes section and may still show a balance and payment due. Because this can be damaging to your score, this is the first thing to remedy. Do so by sending a letter to the Bureau asking for verification of the account. When it comes back verified, send them another letter pointing out that it was improperly verified and demand that it be removed. Be sure to include your bankruptcy paperwork to prove it was included in your bankruptcy. This may help in the removal of the account from the public record.

Third-Party Information Sellers

TransUnion, Equifax, and Experian, the three major credit bureaus, all purchase their information from several third-party information sellers. The top five information selling companies are LexisNexis, ARS, Sage Stream, Innovis, and Pacer. Under the FCRA, these companies are considered CRA's. They must therefore abide by regulations and guidelines outlined in the FCRA.

As a consumer, you may freeze your accounts with data furnishing companies. By doing so, you make it, so the bureaus are unable to verify account information. Despite this, the bureaus often claim that they verified the information with the courts when, in fact, they have not. Courts do not verify public records. This constitutes a gross violation of your rights in the verification process. The next section will help to handle such violations by outlining the steps for you to follow.

Step by step Walkthrough

Step One - Remove and Correct Accounts

Step 1 is to follow the verification and validation procedures previously explained to address and remove accounts listed on your report as "included in bankruptcy." Then also correct accounts that should have been included in the bankruptcy category, but were not.

Step Two - Freeze Your LexisNexis Report

You can freeze your LexisNexis account in one of two ways. First, check their website to see if there are forms provided. If so, fill them out and mail them. If there are no forms, send a letter directly and request a security freeze on your account. Do not proceed to the next step until you have received a response.

Step Three - Ask the Bureau to Verify

Compose a letter stating that it has come to your attention that some information in your bankruptcy is misreported and request verification. Make it clear that you are aware of the 30-day requirement for their response. If you receive a response from the Bureau stating that the information has been verified, move on to step four.

Step four - Court Verification

If you receive a response from the bureaus stating they have verified the information with the court, it is time to compose a letter to the court to inquire if they verify public records like bankruptcies. The court will likely reply that it does not verify such information. Send the court's reply to the bureaus and demand that removal of the information for the Bureau's failure to verify information properly.

Step five - Request Method of Verification

Section 611 of the FCRA requires, upon your request, that the bureaus furnish you with the methods they used to verify the account. They get upwards of 20,000 such requests a day and often cannot meet the demand, causing them to be unable to respond within the required fifteen days. If they do not, you have grounds to take legal action.

Step Six - File a Complaint with The Consumer Financial Protection Bureau

When the bureaus do not respond with the method of verification, or they do not respond in time, it is now within your rights to go to consumerfinance.gov and file a complaint. Be sure to include all of your correspondence. Print a hard copy of that complaint and mail it to the bureaus, along with a letter demanding the removal of the improperly verified public record. Make it clear to them that you feel your rights were violated under the FCRA. Inform them that they can rectify this by deleting the record before filing a small claims lawsuit against them.

Step seven - File a Small Claims Lawsuit

If, after following Step 11, the bureaus still refuse to remove the information, it is within your rights to initiate a small claims lawsuit in response to their violation. If you decide not to go further, rest assured that it is still possible to build better credit after a bankruptcy by following the methods outlined in this book.

STEP TWELVE - SETTLING REMAINING ACCOUNTS

Because not all accounts will be removed from your report, this section will explain how to settle those accounts for less money.

The goal for lenders and collection agencies is to recoup what they can. Because they would rather get partial payment instead of no payment, they will often settle for less than what you owe. This can be done through a settlement offer, which will be explained in the next few pages. The goal of the chapter is to provide you with the necessary tools to successfully negotiate a settlement offer.

The Settlement Offer

When creating a settlement offer, it is essential to follow a few steps to protect yourself. Keep in mind that lenders and debt collectors would rather get partial payment than nothing at all. Use a settlement offer after you've had an account removed, to settle in exchange for removal, or to just settle the account so it will not continue to damage your score.

All steps of a settlement offer should be completed in writing. Verbal agreements are not enough to protect you. Once you have agreed on a settlement offer, be sure to save all the correspondence to protect yourself in case they try to collect the remaining balance. Include a clause prohibiting the creditor from selling the remaining debt to a third party.

In the next few pages, we will discuss the process of settling your debt.

Settlement Request

The first step to settling your accounts is to compose a letter requesting a settlement agreement. The agreement needs to be done in writing to prevent the creditor from trying to sell or collect on remaining debt after the agreement is made. In your settlement letter, request that the credit make an offer to settle the debt. It is important to have the creditor initiate the offer to give you a point from which to negotiate and to prevent you from offering too much. While it is acceptable to make an emotional plea in your offer, remember the main point is to remind the creditor that if you file for bankruptcy, they will get no payment at all. It is in their best interest to settle.

Counter - Offer

Sometimes settlement offers from creditors are unreasonably high. Any offer over 60% meets that criteria. Your response to such an offer should be to remind the creditor that you may consider filing for bankruptcy because your financial situation or budget does not allow for such large settlement amounts. Point out that in the case of bankruptcy, only lenders who make low settlement offers are the ones to get paid. Then counter with an offer of 30%. This hopefully will result in a counteroffer from the lender somewhere in between 30% and their original offer, which is your goal.

Accept Offer

Once you have reached a point where you think you have gotten the lowest settlement possible, write a conditional acceptance letter to the creditor, including the fact that you are willing rot accept their higher settlement in exchange for a three to six month time period to pay, deletion from your report upon satisfactory payment and an agreement not to resell the remaining debt.

The best way to ensure the reliability of the agreement is to request that a supervisor with authority to do so sign and return the agreement before you make your first payment.

Once you receive either the signed contract or a letter acknowledging agreement to those terms, make your payments as agreed and watch your credit score dramatically increase even more!

LETTER INDEX

Letter #1

Client's Name

Client's Address

Credit Bureau

Bureau's Address

Date

To Whom It May Concern:

While reviewing my free copy of my credit report recently, I noticed that some information in the consumer information section needs some correcting and updating. I am requesting that you update the following information: (fill in what you want corrected here). All of my creditors have been provided with the correct personal information by me. If they are reporting anything other than the correct information, they are in violation of the FCRA requirement to report true and accurate information.

Since it is my understanding that you are ALSO required to report true and accurate information, you are also required to correct this information. Please correct my personal information to ONLY reflect the following and delete the other erroneous information.

I am aware of the FCRA requirement that the three credit bureaus are also required to report true and accurate information. Please correct my personal information to include only the following and delete any other inaccurate information.

Name: Joe Schmoe

DOB - 01-01- 01

SSN: 123-45-6789

Address: 123 This Street, Somewhere MD 12345

Also, I request that my telephone numbers not be listed. Please correct the information I have requested and send me a new copy of my report at the above address.

Client's Name

Printed SSN: (Insert SSN)

Enc: Copy of License, Social Security Card and Utility Bill

Thank you for your time and attention to this matter,

Letter #2

»» ——————— ««

Client's Name

Client's Address

Credit Bureau

Bureau's Address

Date

To Whom This May Concern:

On (insert date), I sent a written request to you asking for my personal information to be corrected and update.

Please let this letter serve as a reminder that it is not only the creditors' responsibility but also yours to report only true and accurate information.

My creditors have received my updated personal information and should not report anything other than the information listed below. If there is any erroneous information still remaining in my credit file from my creditors, I demand that you delete their reports from my file.

Furthermore, the following inaccurate information is still listed on my report. This will be my final request for you to correct the information before I proceed with filing a complaint and possibly initiate legal action.

Please delete the following information:

1)

2)

3)

I look forward to your timely response. Please include a copy of my updated report to reflect the changes you make.

Client's Name

Printed SSN: (Insert SSN)

Enc: Copy of License, Social Security Card and Utility Bill

Letter #3

Client's Name

Client's Address

Credit Bureau

Bureau's Address

Date

To Whom This May Concern:

I recently applied for and was denied credit due to the number of inquiries on my credit report. My credit file has been reviewed through a third-party credit monitoring service, and I am alarmed by the number of inquiries I do not recognize. The inquiries in questions are:

- Name of Company and Date of Inquiry
- Name of Company and Date of Inquiry

The FCRA requires credit bureaus to only report true and accurate information. Inquiries into my credit must be for a permissible purpose and require my written permission. I request that you open an investigation into the inquiries I have listed above.

Unless I am provided with documentation of permissible purpose and verification of my written permission for these inquiries within 30 days of receipt of this letter, I request that you remove the unverifiable information as required by the FCRA.

Because I have been denied credit for the last 60 days, the FCRA also requires that I receive an additional free copy of my credit report. Please provide the copy of my report along with the following information for each inquiry listed:

- Permissible Purpose
- Verification of Permission to Inquire - bearing my signature
- Name of the person at your company who verified with the creditor
- Name of the person at the Creditor's Company who provided the information

Thank you in advance for the time spent providing this information. I look forward to reviewing it upon receipt.

Sincerely,

Client's Name

Printed SSN: (Insert SSN)

Enc: Copy of License, Social Security Card and Utility Bill

Letter # 4

»» ———————— ««

Client's Name

Client's Address

Lender's Name

Lender's Address

Date

To Whom This May Concern:

In a recent review of my credit file, I was disturbed to find an inquiry made by your company on (insert date). I do not recall giving your company written authorization to pull my credit file.

The FCRA requires creditors to report only true and verifiable information. I request that you provide me with documentation of permissible purpose, as well as written authorization from me that you had a right to view my report.

In the absence of permissible purpose or verification provided to me within 30 days of the receipt of this letter, you are required to remove the information from my file. I respectfully request that you do so.

Please provide me with the following information regarding your inquiry:

- Permissible Purpose

- Verification of Permission to Inquire - bearing my signature

If you cannot provide me with the requested documentation within 30 days of receipt of this letter, I respectfully request that you remove the inquiry from my credit file.

Thank you for your time in reviewing this inquiry. I look forward to reviewing your response and will be in touch after receiving it.

Client's Name

Printed SSN: (Insert SSN)

Letter #5

»» ———————— ««

Client's Name

Client's Address

Credit Bureau

Bureau's Address

Date

To Whom This May Concern:

Thank you for your response regarding opening an investigation of erroneous inquiries in my credit file. It is clear from your response that you would like me to address this matter to the lender in question. However, under the FCRA, you are responsible for completing the investigation and ensuring that the information in my file is true and accurate. Because you have not honored my request within the 30 days required, I am now requesting that you remove the below-listed inquiries from my file within 15 days of receipt of this letter.

- Name of Company and Date

- Name of Company and Date

- Name of Company and Date

- Name of Company and Date

If upon review of my file after 15 days, I do not find that these inquiries have been removed, I will seek to file a complaint with the Consumer Financial Protection Bureau, as well as the Federal Trade Commission for willful ignorance of my protected consumer rights.

I may also choose to file a small claims lawsuit against your company.

I have attached a copy of my letter dated (insert date) and your response (insert date). You have until (insert date 15 days from the date your client received a response) to delete the erroneous inquiries from my file.

Thank you in advance for your time and attention to this matter. I look forward to receiving and reviewing your response.

Client's Name

Printed SSN: (Insert SSN)

Enc: Copy of License, Social Security Card and Utility Bill

Letter #6

»» ———————— ««

Client's Name

Client's Address

Lender's Name

Lender's Address

Date

To Whom This May Concern:

Thank you for your response to my letter date (insert date) regarding the erroneous inquiry reported in my credit file by your company.

The FCRA requires that you only report true and accurate information and requires that you have a permissible purpose and my written permission to conduct an inquiry into my credit file. I requested that you provide me written evidence of both that demonstrates your right to review my file.

Since you have not provided me with the requested information, or have not done so within the 30 days legally allotted to you, I request that you remove the inquiry from my file within 15 days of receipt of this letter.

If, on the 15th day, I have not received a written response from you fulfilling my request, I am prepared to file complaints with the Consumer Financial Protection Bureau, the Federal Trade Commission, the Attorney General's Office for your willful disregard of my consumer rights. In addition, I am prepared to file a small claims lawsuit against you.

This matter can be easily resolved by your company by simply removing the inquiry from my file, rather than having to resolve complaints filed and appear in court.

Thank you for your time and consideration in resolving this matter. I look forward to prompt receipt of your response.

Client's Name

Printed SSN: (Insert SSN)

Letter #7

Client's Name

Client's Address

Lender's Name

Lender's Address

Date

To Whom This May Concern:

In a recent review of my credit report, it came to my attention that you have reported several late payments. They are listed below.

- insert date

- insert date

The payment dates listed do not match the records I have kept. I am requesting that you send me a copy of my transaction history from (date 3 months prior to the first late payment) to (insert date 2 months after the last late payment date).

If you cannot provide me with the requested transaction history in the next 30 days, I respectfully request that the payments be updated and categorized as on time. It is my understanding that if you are unable to validate that the information you are reporting as true and accurate, then you must update or remove it.

I appreciate the time you will take to look into this, and I will look for your response in the next 30 days.

Client's Name

Printed SSN: (Insert SSN)

Letter #8

»» ———————— ««

Client's Name

Client's Address

Lender's Name

Lender's Address

Date

To Whom This May Concern:

I am writing about a late payment reported in my credit file on (insert date) for my (insert company name) account. I understand my responsibility to make payments on time and take my financial obligations seriously. Unfortunately, during the time period when the payment was due, I had (insert circumstance that caused you to miss a payment - hospital stay, family emergency, injury, job loss, etc.)

Aside from this unforeseen and unavoidable circumstance, my payment history has been excellent. I plan to apply for (insert loan type: personal, auto, home) and realize that a missed payment on my credit report could damage my ability to qualify.

One late payment does not reflect my credit worthiness and commitment to repaying my debts. I am humbly requesting that you make a goodwill adjusting to remove the late payment from (insert date) from my credit report. Your willingness to do so would be greatly appreciated.

To prevent a late payment in the future, I am willing to sign up for auto-pay to keep my credit in good standing.

Thank you for your consideration.

Client's Name

Printed SSN: (Insert SSN)

Letter #9

Client's Name

Client's Address

Credit Bureau

Bureau's Address

Date

To Whom This May Concern:

During a recent review of my credit report, I was alarmed to realize that there are multiple accounts that I am unable to match to any debts I am aware of owing. Would you please verify these accounts to help me understand why they are appearing on my credit report?

Here is a list of all the information I could find on my report, though the account numbers are only partials. I am unclear about where to get the rest of the information I need.

1) Creditor Name claims I owe (amount) and was last reported on (date) under account number (number including the ****).

2) Creditor Name claims I owe (amount) and was last reported on (date) under account number (number including the ****).

If the above-listed creditors cannot verify any and all of the information, I demand that the account be removed immediately.

Thank you for your time and attention to this matter. It is my goal to resolve this issue as soon as possible. Please respond within 30 days.

I have attached a copy of my license, social security card, and a utility bill to prove my identity and address. According to your website, these are an acceptable form of identification.

I am keeping records of our correspondence so that I will be prepared for any legal steps I may need to take if you are unable to verify these accounts within the thirty days.

Sincerely,

Name

Social Security Number

Address

Letter #10

»» ———————— ««

Client's Name

Client's Address

Credit Bureau

Bureau's Address

Date

To Whom This May Concern:

I wrote a letter to you on (insert date) requesting that you investigate several of my accounts. I have attached that letter, the same forms of identification and address I originally sent, as well as a copy of your response that claims I didn't send the correct identifying information. I have also attached a copy of the proper forms of identification listed on your website.

Because I have provided proof that your claim that I did not send proper identification is false, the 30-day deadline to complete your investigation still applies. My letter was sent on (insert date of the original letter), so you have 30 days from that date to complete your investigation. The responsibility lies with you to complete the investigation.

I am looking forward to a successful resolution as a result of your investigation and am fully aware of my legal rights as a consumer. I am keeping careful records of all of our correspondence to prepare myself if legal action on my part needs to be taken.

Warm Regards

Name

Social Security Number

Address

Letter #11

Client's Name

Client's Address

Credit Bureau

Bureau's Address

Date

To Whom This May Concern:

I wrote a letter to you dated (insert date) asking you to investigate some accounts on my credit report. I have attached a copy of the letter, with the same forms of identification, as well as my address. I received your response stating that you were unable to find any accounts with the information I provided. Since I have proven that I provided the correct information, it is unclear to me why the investigation has not moved forward.

I am emphasizing my personal information below in large letters to ensure you understand it clearly.

MY NAME IS (INSERT) MY ADDRESS IS (INSERT), AND MY SOCIAL SECURITY NUMBER IS (INSERT)

It is my expectation that you locate my file and investigation the accounts in question within the 30-day period outlined in the FCRA. The 30-day period began the day you received my first letter. Your assertion that I did not provide the proper information is untrue. I am expecting resolution of this issue and am well aware of my rights as a consumer.

I am looking forward to receiving the results of the investigation I requested. The erroneous information in my credit file is damaging my credit. Because of my knowledge of my rights as a consumer, I am aware that the responsibility lies on you to resolve this issue. I have kept a detailed record of all our correspondence to prepare me for any legal action I may need to take if this issue is not resolved.

Sincerely,

Name

Social Security Number

Address

Letter #12

Client's Name

Client's Address

Credit Bureau

Bureau's Address

Date

To Whom This May Concern:

On (insert date of the original letter), I wrote you a letter requesting that you investigate some account in my credit file. Attached please find a copy of the letter, along with the forms of identification I submitted. I received your response stating your belief that the letter was written by someone other than me. This response only serves to delay the investigation I requested. I provided my signature and the proper identification documents, as outlined on your website.

If there is another method for verifying my identity that you require, you have failed to communicate that to me. Therefore, I demand that you continue with the investigation I requested. I have followed all procedures correctly and know my rights under the law as a consumer. Your assertion that someone else composed and sent the letter has made the 30-day time period shorter. As you are well aware, the investigation must be completed within 30 days from the date you received the original letter.

The erroneous information on my credit report is really damaging my credit through no fault of my own. I have done my part to become an educated consumer and have a working knowledge of the laws that protect me. I wish to be treated as such.

Please be advised that if you continue to stall or refuse to investigate, I am prepared to file a complaint with the Consumer Financial Protection Bureau and initiate a small claims suit. I have kept detailed records of all of our correspondence to prepare me to file the complaint and initiate the small claims suit. This situation can be resolved simply by your completing the investigation within the 30-day deadline you are required to meet.

Sincerely,
Name
Social Security Number
Address

Letter #13

Client's Name

Client's Address

Credit Bureau

Bureau's Address

Date

To Whom This May Concern:

I wrote a letter on (insert date) requesting that you investigate some accounts in my credit file. Attached please find a copy of the letter, as well as the required forms of identification listed on your website. I have received your response stating that my request is frivolous. I would like you to account for and explain the reasons for this determination. As a consumer, I am aware of my right to dispute any information in my credit file that I do not recognize. As a credit bureau, you have the responsibility to investigate and report to me.

It is unclear to me why you feel you have the legal right to deny my request for an investigation. I am prepared to exercise my right under the law to file a complaint against you with the Consumer Financial Protection Bureau. I am also prepared to file a small claims lawsuit against you if my request for an investigation continues to be denied. My right to take both of these actions is outlined in the FCRA.

As you are well aware, once a request is made to investigate a consumer file, that investigation must be completed within 30 days of the original letter. I expect that time period to be honored. My original letter was written on (insert date).

Because the erroneous information in my credit file is damaging my credit through no fault of my own, I expect you to fulfill your responsibility under the law to complete the investigation promptly and to respect my rights as an educated consumer.

Please be advised that if you continue to stall or refuse to investigate, I am prepared to file a complaint with the Consumer Financial Protection Bureau and initiate a small claims suit. I have kept detailed records of all correspondence in this matter and plan to use it to take legal action if necessary.

Warm Regards

Name

Social Security Number

Address

Letter #14

Client's Name

Client's Address

Credit Bureau

Bureau's Address

Date

To Whom This May Concern:

On (insert date of the original letter), I wrote a letter requesting that you investigate some accounts in my credit file. Attached please find a dated copy of the letter. I have received your response dated (insert date you received the response), stating that the account was verified. However, I feel certain that this account is not valid and should be deleted from my file.

I am exercising my rights under FCRA 611 (a) (7) and requesting that you provide a complete description of all methods employed to investigate my dispute. Please include contact information for each company with whom you verified the information, the names of the individuals with whom you spoke, and all correspondence between your Bureau and each company.

If you cannot provide me with the requested information within 15 days, I demand that the accounts be deleted from my credit file. If they are not removed, I will take legal action. I am well aware of my rights as a consumer and have kept detailed records of all our correspondence so that I can provide evidence in the form of a formal complaint and/or small claims lawsuit.

I look forward to your prompt response to this matter.

Sincerely,

Name

Social Security Number

Address

Letter #15

»» ———————————— ««

Client's Name

Client's Address

Credit Bureau

Bureau's Address

Date

To Whom This May Concern:

On (insert date of the original letter), I requested in writing that you investigate some accounts in my credit file. You responded on (insert date you received the response) that the account information had been verified. On (insert date you requested a description of procedures for the investigation), I wrote a letter requesting that you provide me with a description of your investigative procedures. Your Bureau failed to (insert "provide the information requested" OR "did not provide a sufficient description of your investigative procedures").

Because your company has not honored my request and my rights that are protected by consumer law, I have decided to file a formal complaint. It is unacceptable to have my request and rights as an educated consumer ignored. The erroneous information in my file has caused personal and familial distress and prevented me from (insert situation: getting a mortgage, auto loan, obtain a rental property, etc.).

Attached, please find copies of all my letters on this matter, your responses, and finally, my complaints to the Consumer Financial Protection Bureau, the Federal Trade Commission, the Better Business Bureau, and the Attorney General.

I am demanding that you remove the accounts you have failed to verify. If this does not happen, I plan to initiate a small claims action. I have kept detailed records of all our correspondence and plan to present it as evidence to the court.

These legal actions can be avoided if you remove all the accounts in question within 10 days of receiving this letter.

I will look forward to your prompt response.

Sincerely,

Name

Social Security Number

Address

Letter #16

»» ———————— ««

Client's Name

Client's Address

Credit Bureau

Bureau's Address

Date

To Whom This May Concern:

In our repeated correspondence, it has become evidently clear to me that you do not plan to honor my rights as a consumer, or the laws that protect me from predatory practices. Because I have kept a detailed record of all our correspondence, I am confident that a judge will rule in my favor.

As such, I have filed a small claims lawsuit against you, and you are now required to appear at:

(Insert Court Name and Address)

On: (Insert Date)

To answer to the following claims:

· Violations of the Fair Credit Reporting Act - including but not limited to Section 611

· Violations of [insert any corresponding state laws if you desire]

I am seeking (insert amount) in damages:

If, between now and the above court date, you correct your records and delete the information in question, I will withdraw the claim. Please contact me at the address listed above to inform me if you decide to take this action.

I look forward to your prompt response.

Sincerely,
Name
Social Security Number
Address

Letter #17

Client's Name

Client's Address

Lender's Name

Lender's Address

Date

To Whom This May Concern:

While recently reviewing my credit report after being denied credit, I was alarmed to find an account misreported by your agency. This is a clear violation of my rights as a consumer, and I would like an explanation for this inaccurate report.

This letter is regarding account # (insert #), which you allege that (insert applicable debt situation). I am requesting that you provide me with evidence proving this account belongs to me. A copy of a bill is unacceptable evidence; I would like evidence that will hold up in court, such as a contract bearing my signature.

In the absence of a contract bearing my signature, the debt you claim I owe in invalid. If you cannot provide me with proof that I agreed to pay this debt, I am requesting that you immediately remove the report from my credit file.

As I'm sure you are aware, the regulation outlined in the FDCPA and FCRA requires you to perform your due diligence by providing evidence of my ownership of this debt or delete the account. I am well aware of my rights as a consumer and am prepared to take legal action using the record; I have carefully kept a record of all our correspondence.

I will expect your response within 30 days. Thank you for your time and attention to the matter.

Sincerely,

Name

Social Security Number

Address

Letter #18

»» ———————— ««

Client's Name

Client's Address

Lender's Name

Lender's Address

Date

To Whom This May Concern:

In response to your letter dated (insert date) that claims I allegedly owe (insert amount and account number), I would like documentation proving that I agreed to this debt. I would also like an explanation of the procedures you followed to validate this debt.

Please provide me with a description of the procedures you used to verify my agreement to this debt, along with the name and phone number of the employee who verified the account so that I may speak with him/her about the validation process.

Because you have not provided me with verification of your procedures, my rights as a consumer are being violated. As you know, your failure to provide me with the requested evidence is in violation of the FCRA and the FDCPA. You have reported unverifiable and unvalidated information in my credit file despite your failure to provide the verification I requested.

Because of your lack of action, I am suffering from financial and emotional stress. I am demanding that you remove the item from my credit file. I expect a response from you stating that you are removing the account from my credit file and ceasing collection activity.

Because the 30-day deadline for you to provide verification has passed and you have failed to do so, you are now required by law to remove the item from my credit file.

Sincerely,
Name
Social Security Number
Address

Letter #19

»» ———————— ««

Client's Name

Client's Address

Lender's Name

Lender's Address

Date

To Whom This May Concern:

I wrote you a letter on (insert date) requesting verification of the following account:

Account Name and Account Number

Amount Owed:

According to the certified mail receipt, you received this letter on (insert date).

You have failed to respond to my request within the 30-day time period required by law. You are now in violation of FDCPA. You are now required to remove the account from my credit file.

I would like the account removed within 15 days of receipt of this letter. If this does not occur, I plan to file a small claims lawsuit against you. I have kept meticulous records of our correspondence and am confident that I have met the burden of proof needed to win the claim. A simpler and less time-consuming resolution would be for you to simply remove the account from my credit file before the 15-day deadline. This would be a less costly solution for you.

I look forward to your prompt response.

Sincerely,

Name

Social Security Number

Address

Letter #20

Client's Name

Client's Address

Lender's Name

Lender's Address

Date

To Whom This May Concern:

Through our repeated correspondence, it is clear to me that you do not intend to honor my rights as a consumer, nor do you intend the honor that laws that protect me from predatory practices. I have kept a detailed record of all our correspondence and feel confident that a judge will rule in my favor.

As such, I have filed a small claims lawsuit against you, and you are now required to appear at:

(Insert Court Name and Address)

On: (Insert Date)

To answer to the following claims:

- Violations of the Fair Credit Reporting Act

- Violations of the Fair Debt Collection Practice Act

- Defamation of Character

- Violations of [insert any corresponding state laws if you desire]

I am seeking (insert amount) in damages:

If, between now and the above court date, you decide to correct your records and delete the information in question, please contact me at the address listed above, and I will withdraw the claim immediately.

I will look forward to your quick response.

Sincerely,

Name

Social Security Number

Address

Letter #21

Client's Name

Client's Address

Lender's Name

Lender's Address

Date

To Whom This May Concern:

In an effort to straighten out my financial affairs, I am requesting information from you regarding an account I used to have with you for a (insert make and model of car). I am asking for the following information:

- Original Installment Sales Contract

- Transaction History

- Amount Owed and explanation of any letters sent during the repossession process to clarify amounts I allegedly owe.

I am aware that under the FDCPA, you are required to provide the requested information to me within 30 days of receipt of this letter. Time is of the essence, and any effort on your part to get the information to me sooner would be greatly appreciated.

Thank you for your time and attention to this matter. I will be in touch once I have received and reviewed the information. Due to a move, my address is different than what is printed on my license. Please respond to me at the address listed above.

Client's Name

Printed SSN: (Insert SSN)

Enc: Copy of License

Letter # 22

»» ——————— ««

Client's Name

Client's Address

Lender's Name

Lender's Address

Date

To Whom This May Concern:

I have received the information you sent to me regarding my request for information dated (insert date). I hereby give notice that I am disputing the accounts under Vin # (insert number). The vehicle in question was purchased on or about [insert date], financed by [insert company], repossessed in the state of [insert state], and sold by [insert notice that company/creditor] on or about [insert date].

The following notices were not sent to me after you took possession of the vehicle, as required by (insert state) law. I made a request for these notices on (insert date) that was not honored. I am writing to demand proof that the repossession of the vehicle was legal with the following:

UCC: § 9-506. EFFECT OF ERRORS OR OMISSIONS.

§ 9-611. NOTIFICATION BEFORE DISPOSITION OF COLLATERAL

§ 9-612. TIMELINESS OF NOTIFICATION BEFORE DISPOSITION OF COLLATERAL.

§ 9-613. CONTENTS AND FORM OF NOTIFICATION BEFORE DISPOSITION OF COLLATERAL

You are required to provide me with proof of these notices within 15 days of the receipt of this letter. If the information is not received, then your alleged claim of a deficiency is null and void, and I demand you cease collection efforts and remove the report from my credit file. To do otherwise would violate my protected rights under the FCRA and FDCPA, and I reserve the right to seek damages against all parties, under all available State and Federal statutes and including but not limited to UCC § 9-625 remedies.

I will be tracking this letter through certified mail and expect your response within 15 days of its receipt. If, by the 16th day, I have not received a response or if it has not been removed from my credit file, I will be forwarding all relevant correspondence and documentation to my attorney for review. I am well aware of my rights as a consumer and expect to be treated as such. Please correct the error you made that resulted in a violation of my rights.

Thank you for your time,

Client's Signature

SSN

Client's Name

Client's Address

Letter #23

»———————«

Client's Name

Client's Address

Credit Bureau

Bureau's Address

Date

To Whom This May Concern:

It has recently come to my attention that there is an illegal repossession reporting on my account by (insert lender) under account number (insert account number)

I have repeatedly requested that the lender provide me with proof that they are reporting properly, and they have failed to do so. They are required to send me a notice to cure and a notice of deficiency, and they did neither despite my request that they do so.

They, like you, have only 15 days to respond under the FCRA. 15 days have now passed and they have not provided this evidence. I am now requesting you investigate this account, and if the account is verified by (insert lender) at any point in your process, I request that you send me your method of verification. I am absolutely certain they are reporting illegally.

I would like a complete description of all methods used to investigate my aforementioned dispute. I would this to include a complete list of all documents and correspondence with (insert lender), the name of the person employed by you that contacted (insert lender), and the name of the person contacted at (insert lender). I would like to ask that you not send me one of your template letters; instead, I request a letter outlining the details of my account and your investigative procedures, as I am working to build a case against this lender.

Because my credit score and financial health are a priority to me, I would like to rectify this situation as soon as possible. I fully expect that you will comply with my request since you are required to abide by the regulations outlined in the FCRA and FDCPA to protect me as the consumer. I will look forward to your response in 15 days or less, and I expect to see the item permanently deleted from my file. Thank you for your time and attention to this very urgent matter.

Client signature

SSN ENC: License, SSC, Utility bill,

Copy of your ID requirements from your website.

Conclusion

Everyone is entitled to good credit. I have given you the knowledge and tools you need to correct errors on your credit report and raise your credit score. Now it is up to you to take the steps needed to obtain your best score. Remember if you need help, I am here for you.

About the Author

Dr. Derek A. Smith, Ed.D, MBA, MS, Speaker, Author, and Educator

Derek A. Smith is the president of Simplified Financial Services LLC.

Derek regularly appears on various news programs and conducts regular webinars, podcasts, blogs, and public talks.

Derek has a Doctorate Degree in Organizational Leadership, an MBA and several Masters degrees. He studied financial planning at Bryant University, and has certificates in real estate investing from MIT and Cornell universities. He is a

Certified Personal Finance Consultant (CPFC) and Certified Financial Education Instructor – Financial Literacy Certification (CFEI) through the National Financial Educators Council

Derek is an associate professor at the University of Maryland, University College, Virginia University of Science and Technology, and Excelsior College and has taught business and information technology classes for over 30 years. He is also a Board advisor for several boards.

Derek served in the US Navy, Air Force, and Army for a total of 24 years.

For fun, Derek has practiced martial arts for over 35 years and holds black belts in several martial arts. He also has acted in movies, television, industrial films, and commercials. Derek is available for consulting, training, and speaking engagements. You can contact him at derek@simplifiedfinancialservices.com

Derek lives with his family in Upper Marlboro, Maryland.

www.ingramcontent.com/pod-product-compliance
Lightning Source LLC
Chambersburg PA
CBHW072056150726
47999CB00005B/1795